MY MIND
THE
JOURNEY
THROUGH
LOVE
and the
REST

MY MIND
THE JOURNEY
THROUGH
LOVE
and the
REST

AARON ALLEN

My Mind: The Journey Through Love and the Rest
Copyright © 2015 by Aaron Allen. All rights reserved.

No part of this publication may be reproduced, stored in a retrieval system or transmitted in any way by any means, electronic, mechanical, photocopy, recording or otherwise without the prior permission of the author except as provided by USA copyright law.

This book is designed to provide accurate and authoritative information with regard to the subject matter covered. This information is given with the understanding that
the author is not engaged in rendering legal, professional advice.
Since the details of your situation are fact dependent, you should additionally seek the services of a competent professional.

Cover design by Nino Carlo Suico
Interior design by Caypeeline Casas

Published in the United States of America

ISBN: 978-0-57848-119-7
Poetry / Subjects & Themes / General
14.12.16

CONTENTS

To the Reader…(A Quick Understanding)	7
The First Journey: Love and a Little More	9
First Stop: Love	12
Love	15
Love Story	18
Sad to Say	21
My Love (For Her)	24
The Love of the South	27
A Crown of Thorns, His Love	31
The Love of a Real Jamaican Heritage (A Letter)	35
My Prayer (God Break Me)	37
The Last Love Stop (The Announcement)	42
Pride and Humility (My Testimony)	44
The Love of Good Poetry	46
Last Chapter	48
The Snake and Me…	53
Part 2, The Snake and Me (The Good Sheppard's Help)	56
Part 3, The End to a Short Story (The Snake and Me)	57

A. C. against Aaron: The Heavyweight Fight!!!!	58
The End of the Rest (For Now)	61
The Ballad of Me	68

TO THE READER...
(A Quick Understanding)

Welcome to my Mind and the drama and fun within it I love you, and I haven't met you. (I hope that didn't sound too weird) I want you to take a look at this, and again I don't know you. Maybe I do, maybe I met you. But, it doesn't really matter, you're here. However, you got here. Now, I want you to understand that this is a statement, if you will. The title and the content within this book is a statement. It "Statement" is in mostly letter and poetry form, but the Idea of my mind and all of its interesting stories has been sprawled out here to lead you through a mind that has encountered love, hate and the rest (the rest being explained further as you read). So we will take a peek at the good side and the bad side of a mind and its person, that has found a life of its own through the traumatic and good experiences held within these pages, But I wanted to start with Love. True love. Thanks again…Oh, and don't forget A. C. He made me give him credit too.

—A. C.

Let's start moving forward through this Journey now…

THE FIRST JOURNEY
Love and a Little More

My Mind: Journey of LOVE and the Rest

This journey, hmmm, where do we start?
Well If Love starts from the Heart
Then I'll start from there
But it's really starting within My Mind
No not his mind, it's not smart enough
But my mind is.
And he will never catch up

The doors that lead to this mind is mental
And you have to believe me a little
To see the Love and Insults,
The drama, and the good times
The pride and the humility

A step into the first door,
Starts the journey
But there's so much more to see
That if I took the time to write it all then

There would be only a beginning,
But no end

And I will end
But only to spare you and your time
So remain with me and be faithful
Until the end
Even though there might be some sharp turns
And bends within here, or beyond this entrance

—The Journey via A. C.

Moving on…forward and never backward (message to you)

FIRST STOP
Love

Atlanta: Oh how I LOVE how you raised me.

What can I say, Atlanta
You raised me
Just like my mother
I have Love for you
Okay to Be Honest
I have a lot of Love for my City
Why?
Because you raised me Atlanta
From baby to granddaddy
I grew up in your arms
In your care
Your bad side I saw
Your good side I saw
Your oval shape of 285
Surrounded all of me 95 percent of my life
South Atlanta, to North Atlanta
I learned my people
My blood family to my childhood friends

You birthed some of them
And the others you
Adopted as well
You gave us all an identity
That would rival the other popular cities
Like Detroit, New York, LA, Chicago, and Miami
Shout-out to all my Chicago and Detroit peeps
Sorry again,
That last line was A.C.
He wanted to give those peeps a hello
But back to Atlanta
Where from there I still began to grow

But what does that mean for me?
Nothing really
It just means that I love you
For help raising me,
And hopefully my child
Will get to experience this Great City
I Love you Atlanta

We are STILL MOVING forward… Believe me a little

LOVE

What she did

What she did
She showed me Love
She didn't show me any sexual love
She showed me concern
Concern for my well-being
Which is how Love is defined

She showed me a heart for me
A heart for people, it was pulsating with agitation,
It wanted to burst, but never did
She would often break her heart for others
And then turned and gave me that old broken heart
She was awarded a new heart from the master

But I still had that heart that was a little broken but it still worked
And beggars can't choose
Being that I wanted a better heart
She gave me her old broken heart from the master
That He gave her before the new one

But I was still with the Old heart

As it was dark red with a spoiled tomato look
It pulsated hard, it would hurt
But nevertheless
She gave me that heart
Now with Her new one that is
She shared it, showed it, never shunned it
So her new Heart was my broken Love
God broke my heart through her
God saved me through her
God showed me his Love and Mercy through her

SHE WAS IN MY LIFE FOR ONLY ONE REASON
TO SHOW ME GOD'S LOVE
THANK YOU
I LOVE YOU

—A. C.

Still moving, Sorry

LOVE STORY

I remember a young girl
Who looked like a model
You know, the coke bottle type
Typical. Tight. Touching.
You get the picture
All the boys wanted her
Until we hooked up
But who would know
It would only get deeper
All the time she would hit me with a text message
Or on the receiver
From the modeling
To the music videos
Her ego began to blow up in my face
Such a beautiful disgrace
So babe lets go
One more time
For old times' sake
Oh no she just rejected that offer
Okay…
Moving on…

On To the next
Who stole my heart
but It's funny how I thought
That we would never fall apart
Then when I tried to
Get her back
OH no
Who's this new jack?
It don't matter
Too late…
Crap
How could you do me like that?
Mmm, it was nice
But maybe your cuteness
Caused lust
And not Love
Mmm, that was nice
It was just right
How can you forget?
Those three a.m. morning nights
Until you fell asleep
Or the movie with long mall walks
But let's rewind
I mean fast forward
I remember the time
When I met a lovely college freshman
Who all the guys looked at as fresh meat

We started talking casually
And it became formal
Then to dress clothes
Now were serious about our company
So hating us together
Became there job
And you split like a couple
Now I'm single
Oh well
The well is never dry
I know, but she blamed me
Talking about their my friends
But I didn't know them
Well not really
But with her stuff
She wasn't discreet
Oops, did that slip?
No I wrote it down
So it might last longer
Ahh, girls
First they give you their heart
Then they take it back
They also say it's my fault
And I regrettably regret this
Ha-ha, but really
This is just my love story

—A. C.

SAD TO SAY

Sad to say
That my dear,
I must see you another day
It's getting dark out here tonight
The inner parts of my soul/mind
Are turning an awful grey
The storms of my mind are thundering
From which your love was wondering
Question after question
Thought after thought
Answer after answer
Does she love me?
Or does she not?
Will new feelings for another come about?
Or will my Love for God be my only Devout?
Now I must move on…
Moving… Working… Please hold
Okay back on track
Now my heart is stretched out
To a more oblong shape
And it seems that

There's holes in it
With seemingly hate
But whatever happens
Is probably meant
So I wait

—A. C.

Moving....

MY LOVE (FOR HER)

My love
Look at your beauty
Such a tease
But you're Godly
HE made you perfectly imperfect
I love you, Miss Lady
This writing should have been in red,
Why red?
It shows your power and strength
You are there
When I need you
Emotionally and physically
Mmm, I'm sorry,
There is a thin line here
But between Love and Lust
Because I don't hate
Well, at least you
Maybe the other girls
Or other dudes
Okay ill stop
But there hating too

So tell those hating guys
To go away and her too
No, no, no
Where you going?
Were not done
Not at all
Stop acting
You're not an actress
But you look like it
I do truly love you too
Everything about you
So before you leave
Let's be…

—A. C.

Moving on from Her now, I guess

THE LOVE OF THE SOUTH

I wake up to a familiar smell
The smell of a cooked breakfast
No, not hot cereal, or anything bland
I'm talking about a real somewhat salty smell
Cheesy smell, a more tasteful smell
More distinct
So I wake up in the south
In a cozy pull out coach
South Carolina, not Georgia
Or even my real home, Atlanta
SC, is where I am in this remembrance
Spartanburg to be even more specific
And also more relevant
Where we went for my dad's parents
Mmm, that smell again
Mmm, mmm, mmm

So I get up, get ready and go up the stairs
While laugh in my mind about that thought of alliteration
I just thought of
As I ascend, to the upper room

Where the kitchen is
And where this temporary heaven is
Well at least that what it feels like
Mmm, that smell, that warmth,
That food, that love
Heaven…

I see my father's mother in the small kitchen
Finishing the finished products
I see my grandfather, sitting next to my father
The two men who came directly before me
In the direct line, a thrown
That I now sit on

But that smell, keeps kicking at me
Now the smell turns into a visual
A beautiful visual
Food, southern foods,
A southern breakfast
I love this type of food,
That is before us now
With my sister, my mother, my father, my grandfather, and my grandmother
The table is set
We pray

We thank THE FATHER in heaven
For the goodness of the food we were about to receive
And the visual in my eyes widens
As I open them
I see…

Grits, Cheese Grits,
Sausage links, other meats I can't recall
Other southern delights befall and sit on the table now
But the Cheese grits got me
My favorite, if you didn't already know

But this gourmet breakfast grits
Were made with Love,
Made with the love of the south
Made with a deep tradition that we as southerners share

I don't really know how to describe the taste
Of these Cheese Grits
But it never loses it saltiness
Always good, mmm
So I eat, full now
Mouth closed
But that smell…
Where did it go?

Moving out of that House back home,
and then forward…

A CROWN OF THORNS, HIS LOVE

*(A psalm of praise,
one time for the believer of God)
I love you all*

JESUS!!!
You are wonderful
Beautiful, forgiving, understanding
Soft and gentle, but still all power and authority goes to you
But most of all

You are love, you love,
Because you know
The greatest of these is Love
And who can argue with LOVE
Your Love, from where all humans
Should understand Love

But some say
That you don't exist,
That you're not God's son

That you didn't even die for me,
That you didn't die on a tree

But I don't say,
Anything, I just believe
Because that's what I see,
Believe and know
Because you know my testimony

Where you found me
How you help me out
How you made me more
Distinct and profound

And being that were on this testimony
I remember when I didn't know you
Didn't see you
Like all the rest
But I pray that they

Learn from my mistake
Because I was one of them
Not really caring,
Not really believing

But now I see your true Love and forgiveness
And I have become your TRUE witness
No matter what Pharisees and other people say
And hopefully will see my praise and realness of faith
So Thank You Jesus!!!

—A. C. (with all love and respect to you)

Stumbled, but HE helped me now,
and now we're still moving forward...

THE LOVE OF A REAL JAMAICAN HERITAGE
(A Letter)

Dear, Charles Allen

Hi, Grandpa. Thanks for bearing three wonderful women. I love you and them, and their whole family. Because whoever is their and your family is also mine. I love them all. But your eldest daughter is my mother. When I was little, I remember her and my aunts (even to this day), speaking in broken English. Even in their new age Jamaican accent, and with their childhood being in America. But push comes to shove; they got it from you because you are Jamaican. So my sister and I grew up with that and imitated the accent really good if I say so myself. At my Pre-school, in Atlanta a few times for the schools international day, my mom would make rice and jerk chicken. And recently I was told by a Jamaican and already knew that within the Jamaican heritage as far as the food is concerned we "jerk" everything. That's funny, but to the outside reader they might not understand that, but they can ask a Jamaican or look it up.

Nevertheless, I barely remember you, except for that one memory when you smiled at me, with the spirit of approval. I remember the story from my mother and her sisters; I want to actually meet your Jamaican son, (my half uncle) to see if he looks like me or my other male cousins. Shout out to them too. Because there are only 4 known grandsons, one grand-daughter, and you now have we had three great grandchildren. But I'm doing good learning more about you and our Jamaican heritage. But now I understand who I am, why I act the way I do, and why I look the way I do, and 25 percent of that comes from you. Thank you for my mother, and her family. And again, I love them all as well you. So you and your Son in Law (my father), rest in peace, or as we say now days Rest in Jesus.

—Thank you with Love, your Grandson, Aaron (A.C.)

MY PRAYER
(God Break Me)

God break me
Then fix me

I love you so much
That I'm love sick

With the flu
Your Love is like a fountain

So when things gets hard for me
I will pray to thee

For strength I need
And that you gave me

Strength for what?
strength to be Aaron and not A.C.
Because when I look into the Mirror
There's the only human that scares me

So break me
Then fix me bigger, better, BUT
Keep me humble always
Even if I ball
In this game I play

This is what I pray
I love you Lord
AMEN

DEDICATION TO MY (EARTHLY) FATHER, FREDDIE ATCHISON
(A Son to Father Eulogy)

Freddie Maurice Atchison, you will always live in Christ (written in 2008, and read at his funeral).

November 1, 2008

I never thought that this day would come, well maybe so soon. However, it couldn't have come at a better time. You might ask why I say this:

LET ME EXPLAIN

You see, eight months ago, my father was blessed with his first beautiful granddaughter, but despite his physical complications his luck didn't stop. Just a few weeks later, I told him that I was going back to college after a year out. And now I grow making my own, life's good. But, as you may know, my father was never a real material person, but when he got his laptop he was overjoyed. That is what his wonderful daughter got him on his last birthday.

So you see, this is why I said what I said. Even though he may had been suffering sometimes with a pain, you on the outside would have never known that because He would stay in his bible, in his prayer, so his spirit would always be good to you. I now know that God called him home because he fulfilled his duty in helping raising a Giant (me).

People say no father wants to bury his own son, but now I know. No son wants to bury his own blood father. Over the past few years my father and I had our bad times but we never stopped dealing with each other in a good way, this is true love. I remember times when my father and I would lay a mat down and watch movies on the floor in the living room, until we fell asleep, good times, father-and-son times. As a matter of fact, just right before he passed, I had rented the old Pink Panther movie and we laughed that night and enjoyed our last night together. I praise God and thank him that my father and I went out on good Godly terms because many people don't get that chance, when someone they love dies.

So I ask you to do me a favor family and friends. If you have any bad feelings for him, please let them go. He's gone now, and he's an angel now, and with the Holy One, resting in Jesus, Our King. AMEN

And to all the Sons with earthly fathers living, I urge you to spend enough time with them because their time is coming, so don't miss your chance at your direct blood line, and your direct love. Your time with them should be cherished and your son is coming so learn from your father, how to be a father.

—A. C. aka Freddieson (had to do it, one time)

THE LAST LOVE STOP
(The Announcement)

Poetry and its Love (quick stop) we are half way through this journey through my mind. Let's keep going, I'm your Apollo, and you can be Dante, but don't worry about Heaven or Hell, not to mention Purgatory. If that's what you remember from Sunday school, none of that is here on earth where you reside. But in my mind you're safe, so let's continue to move forward through this mind of Good and Evil. So hold on, it's about to get a lot more interesting. Believe me…

Moving down a little bit, but it's still moving forward.

PRIDE AND HUMILITY
(My Testimony)

From stages
To behind the walls of a Behavior Center
From publishing
To all the hate
From her Love
To her lust
To where winning now
Is a must
Crowned
Then crushed
Moving forward
Backing up
From driving old schools
To catching a bus
It's all the same
Pride and humility
That is
From the south
To the north
From the heat (I'm hot)

To the cold (I'm cold)
Like Cold springs
Always Drinking out of it
But never thirsty
Eating all day
But still
Always hungry
Eatting like a cow
Still shaped like an ant
I'm a king
And a servant
My Pride
My humility
My testimony

—A. C.

THE LOVE OF GOOD POETRY

This is writing
Not recording
But really the same
Just no music or hook
But the hook is my mind
Are you hooked?

No real aim here
No shot from a barrel
The aim of this?
It's at poetry
No diss

This poetry your reading
You now are now tasting
Taste good, doesn't it?
From your eyes
To your other senses

So like a drug
You want more of

Mmm, more,
More, more, more

No time for anything
Not even time for chores
So like a kid and their candy
You want more
So sweet,
Its sugary sensation
Seemingly sweet
Now and later

But the Love of good poetry is good
Because it cares for you
It cares for your well-being

There's a pack now
And a pack for you later
So get ready
Now and later
And consider the rapper
but keep in mind its STILL my cover

Okay, I'm done,

    —A. C. (sorry he has to have his signed name on it)

LAST CHAPTER

The next, and final, trip: the rest of my mind (Final journey, part 2).

The Journey of the rest

So I open the door for you
You walk in and you see it's a room, my room
It's a normal room, a normal place in my mind
With a couch (for mental rest), lamp (for light), and an old broom
The broom?
I don't know why that's there
I guess it was used for cleaning the craziness up from before
Craziness? You ask
Okay, the nonsense from my recent past
All the dirt from my past that
I have been trying to clean up
For the past year
But I got tired of it and just put that old broom down
Do you see that pen on my living room table?
That's what I have been using more

It—the pen, that is

It helps better with that cleaning up of the past
Because it heals everything really
Even the rest

But let me now turn your attention to this Chest
Here
As you look there
Yeah that old, wooden, mysterious chest
Oh and don't ask how it got in My Mind…
You see it's just like
One of those old treasure chests
But it's the best (Sorry A. C. said that)
You can't break it open
That easily
Actually not at all
But…
Oh you want to know what's in this Chest of my treasure?
You really want to know what's in the rest of my mind?
Well, okay, being that you are here now
But I warn you…
Never mind that

'cause you have inquired about it already
Then let's open this Chest of the Rest…
I open it…

A. C. Entertainment (A three-part poem)

Part 1

I walk into a dim lit room
Smiles and frowns
They shake my hand
But as soon I turn around
They stab me…
Right in the spine
Typical…
Should have known
Should have known they weren't friends
But I love them, until the end
I bend but don't break
I shake but never shook or
so don't think I'm timid
So I never hid
But they couldn't wait
And that's their mistake
so I decided to shake and bake
And I got out
Only to come back to that same room
That same surroundings
That same troubling
So I see the enemies
But now they're under me
As always

Part 2, A. C. Entertainment

Now it's a stage
They are excited and enraged
With the fire of my popularity and fame
Because I come right every year
With great entertainment and tears
I smile to the fans
But they don't know this man
How do I feel?
Good enough
Just getting by
Just getting money
No more getting fried
But you could still fry that old beef
But we will leave that to beaver
Cause I used to have a beef cleaver
Sorry, I do eat meat for real
No fakes or false orders
No more movies, No more spoofs, No more Jokes
No games, no more games, No coach

Such a shame, but who's to blame?
Me? Them?
I don't know, and there's no clue
Unless you find one
But until then…
Cold case…

Part 3, the final show of A. C. Entertainment

Now I'm every where,
On your Kindle,
On your screen
On your magazine
On your everything
Now you see me
And you will
Always see me
The star

—A. C.

THE SNAKE AND ME...
Part 1

Let me explain an interesting story, through poetry
I was in the grass one day
Just enjoying the soft grass and the beautiful Son
Ignore past, present, future problems
I sensed him though, I sensed the snake
But only a little bit, not worrying about the bite
But soon the bite would come
The little voice said he was coming
The voice said
"Don't fear him, don't go running"
But I told the comforter
"I'm not afraid"
But the comforter, kept repeating what he said
Until the snake finally came through the think grass
Unannounced, unwanted, unneeded
But this time he raised his arrowhead like head
And fangs sharper than any sword that a roman soldier might have had
A dark green, with deep dark beady eyes... The only real and pure evil

(Bear with me people, don't worry)

He first would hiss at me
Saying, "Ssssstop before I bite"
But I didn't hear it
Because now, I was inviting others
To join me in the green pasture
And he didn't like me helping people get to the pasture
So he didn't like it
The snake, that is
He got mad
I laughed,
And then he raised his head higher
Out of the blades of grass
I now saw his full, scaly body
Bigger than I expected
Bigger scales, bigger body, darker (his spirit was darker)
More Scaly, a wider body, darkish green
He gleamed in the sun,
As if he was an angel of light
But he wasn't, maybe a demon of darkness
No definitely he was evil and not an angel at all

He brutally bit a brother, than bit a sister
But I was too prideful to see it before
When I could have stopped it before
Then I mourned

And in my humility now, he sank his sharp fangs into my leg,
Into my mind, well, I guess he didn't lie this time
And this time only he didn't lie
At this moment,
No walking away now, no leaving now, no escape
The grass began to wither, and all the other people left
Including the sun
Now its dark, his turf (the snake's turf)
No grass, well, at least it was fake and artificial

This was the snake's heaven
And my hell

PART 2,
THE SNAKE AND ME
(The Good Sheppard's Help)

Come back, breakout the comforter said
No more chains, I saw them fall
The good Sheppard came to me
Where I was
Then he came and healed my legs
So I got up and walked away
Still hurting a little though
But my moving was slowly, but still surely moving forward
And this angered to see my soul
Finally leaving his nine deeper holes
Now the good Sheppard was there
To crush the head and kill the snake
I knew the Good Sheppard
And his power over the snake
So he helped me, now the snake was dead
But his evil spirit some times resonated
For a higher purpose of the good Sheppard's boss

PART 3,
THE END TO A SHORT STORY
(The Snake and Me)

So now the comforter
Stays with me
Standing there, fighting there, protecting me from the snake
He was the true angel or dove of light
So we thank him and God, amen

A. C. AGAINST AARON: THE HEAVYWEIGHT FIGHT!!!!
(Get Tickets!!!)

Part 1 (The Conversation, Within My Mind)

Setting: A Workout Room Within My Mind

Aaron (me): Who are you?

A. C.: I am you, but the bigger, better, smart, and more handsome version of you (laughs)

Me: (lowered eyebrows, a minor frown) Wait, what?

A. C.: I'M YOUUUUU, BOY! Don't worry about it, bruh, cause afta tonight you won't exist anymore, Aaron. With all your lame humility. I'm the greatest, not your lame book. Now you know people, your people love me. Only because they want me more cause they love my pride. This world loves my pride, and you're lame with all your humility.

Me: Bu—

A. C.: Not done! Ha ha, I'm the best, so you need to be thanking me, other than thanking me. For what? FOR GIVING YOU PRIDE, AARON! I got rid of those lame few people who tried to hate on you by crushing their egos, fame, and their hate towards me, or I guess us. It didn't matter if they were rappers, or just some lame that tried to take your spot at the top. Look around, Aaron, you should be thanking me.

Me: But—

A. C.: I know what you're going to say, you're going to say, Love your enemies. Lame, lame. LAME. They lame too. You enemies are lame that's what I was talking about. Ha-ha, anyway, I took them all out, even the slow people who tried to catch up with you.

Me: Okay, you did all that, I'll give you that, but why are you still here? There's no one here but us.

A. C.: Yeah, yeah, yeah, but you need me for life, well, if you want to be successful in this world, again, they Love me, they enjoy me, I entertain them. NO, wait, you're no longer me, I will take you out when this fight comes up in the next book that really stars me, and not just a feature in this book. That's why I wanted more from you now in this book.

Me: Well, we will see…

—Aaron via A. C.

(Be on the lookout in the next short story, with the full story, A.C./Aaron: The Heavyweight Fight)

THE END OF THE REST
(For Now)

We will now end, with strictly poetry

Fake Thugs (The Alliance)

July 16, 2009, at 1:39 p.m.

I hate false claiming naggers
Straight OG thugs
Claim to be oriental
As American rugs
Give me the truth
Like an antismoking campaign
I'll make your hair fall out
And bring it back like Rogaine
Don't try to fool me
For breakfast eating cereal
Stick to tricks for kids
Before I split your wigs
You talk much talk
but no action
and like a soldier without a war

you're torn
and wish you hadn't been born
you try to copy and keep up
but it was already done and you were too slow
so quit the movements and shows
because you can't rise
so stay low

—Big Man (The Alliance)

My Mind, My Swagger (The Poem)

People say I have a look of an actor,
No, it's just that I look like an actor
But really it's that Denzel swagger
From friends to followers
I'm climbing up the popularity ladder
But hate comes with the territory
Now as I look in to the store
I begin to see that I'm a hot topic
And now trying to find away to stop it
Because I don't need that extra attention
And I got a girl
For that extra affection
Yeah, I know I'm a superstar in their eyes
But its myspace
With no message

With no reply
I'm not being stuck up
That just my luck
How it is
And how it's been
Not meant to offend
Because I don't know you
Whoever you are
Like scrooge with his money
Right now I'm stingy
So bear with me
Smooth, sooth, whatever
That's my real personality
And the haters would say never
Because they are under the weather
Under my storm
They are so sick
From the average clown
To the king
That me
And so now I'm taking back my throne
From him who stole it
Only by mouth though
He never took by forcing me off
But back to the subject
I'm getting fat
No not talking literal size

Only because my top and true potential
I now realize
I should write a few letters
And address them to my enemies
And that means
all of you
So before it's too late
Get a clue

—A. C.

(Just a taste) of true lyrical talent (written in 2011).

"Paranoid Song"
Lyrics

During that long way home
I'm having visions of my name on a head stone
'cause this paranoia and nervousness
Won't leave me head alone
I always feel like someone's watching me
Because I know the other side of life
Still wants me
That slipped, sorry
But you saw it,
So I'll leave it there
And in my dreams they constantly haunt me

My mind is becoming overwhelmed with nightmares
And even though there dreams
I don't think I still think they exist in life
Such a strife
But I wake up and realize I'm safe

Chorus:
I'm scared out of my mind
I don't know what to do
I'm so paranoid
I need to get loose

Verse 2
Just the other night
I had a dream of being killed
Well in my dream
That was their will
And it didn't actually happen
So that's why now
I'm registering this weapon
But who would want to kill me?
I am as funny and friendly
As any good Godly man could be
Well that's what they say about me
I guess all the haters
Want this, want me
They want to take my thrown

And they wanted to be king
But they will NEVER
Nope.
Paranoid.

Come on keep up, tourist, just finish with
me, just one last more visit, I promise.

THE BALLAD OF ME
*(Final Thing in Chest,
the End of the Rest)*

This is where I am
Here and now
I've gone too far
To go back
Lost like a kid

Now I need a navigator
With no car to score
Now my inner head has
Manifested a mess
Scared of what?
Scared of NO MAN

It seems therapy
Is all that matters?
Thoughts of violence
Haunt my sleepless nights

Being well-rounded
Doesn't mix with my hidden agenda
Man…where am I now?
How long has it been?
Why am I still here?
Why all these questions?
You ask?
You rang? Please hold
… (listening, still nothing)
Hello?
What am I doing here again?
I guess I'm running from my problems.
Again…

Was I a good Apollo? You were better than Dante. And now you've seen my Devine Comedy, MY mind, my room, my chest, my Journey through of Love and the rest. Thank you and I wish you the best. Stay blessed, my friend. Oh, and again sorry about this. A. C. wants some more credit… Love You and take a good NAP.
(SHUTS door)
More coming.

—A. C.

CPSIA information can be obtained
at www.ICGtesting.com
Printed in the USA
LVHW020102280120
645025LV00013B/1435